TROOP TRAINING
FOR
LIGHT TANK TROOPS

MILITARY TRAINING PAMPHLET No. 27

The Naval & Military Press Ltd

Prepared under the direction of
The Chief of the Imperial General Staff.

Published by

The Naval & Military Press Ltd

Unit 5 Riverside, Brambleside
Bellbrook Industrial Estate
Uckfield, East Sussex
TN22 1QQ England

Tel: +44 (0)1825 749494

www.naval-military-press.com
www.nmarchive.com

DISTRIBUTION

CONTENTS

INTRODUCTION

SEC.

CHAPTER 1

THE ORGANIZATION AND TRAINING OF A LIGHT TANK CREW

CHAPTER 2

THE FORMATIONS AND MOVEMENT OF A TROOP

CHAPTER 3

TROOP TACTICS

CHAPTER 4

POINTS OF PROCEDURE IN TROOP ACTION

CHAPTER 5

ANTI-GAS

INTRODUCTION

1. The armoured division

1. *The armoured division* consists of :—

Headquarters.

Light armoured brigade, consisting of :—

H.Q. and three light armoured regiments.

Heavy armoured brigade, consisting of :—

H.Q. and three heavy armoured regiments.

Support group, consisting of :—

H.Q.

One Royal Horse Artillery regiment.

One A.A. and anti-tank regiment R.A.

One field squadron, R.E.

One field park troop, R.E.

Two motor battalions.

Armoured division signals.

Administrative services (R.A.S.C., R.A.M.C., R.A.O.C., &c.).

2. *Light armoured brigade*

In the mobile operations which the armoured division is designed to carry out, the functions of the light armoured brigade are, broadly speaking, two-fold :—

   i. *Reconnaissance.* To obtain detailed and accurate information of the enemy's forces.

   ii. *Fighting.* To obtain that information and to prevent the enemy getting information about the main dispositions and movements of our own division ; and to create a situation favourable for the employment of the heavy armoured brigade in a decisive blow.

In general terms, the light armoured brigade exercises these functions by advancing with one or more regiments deployed.

Each regiment consists of a H.Q., two light tank squadrons and one light cruiser squadron.

The forward regiments normally deploy their light tank squadrons in reconnaissance, supporting them by the light cruiser squadron when serious opposition is encountered.

3. *Light tank squadrons*

A light tank squadron consists of a headquarters and five troops, each containing three light tanks.

In reconnaissance the squadron is deployed with the minimum number of troops forward necessary to cover the allotted frontage and with the remaining troops in reserve.

A reserve is essential to enable the squadron leader to increase the power of reconnaissance, to extend the front, or to replace a forward troop which is temporarily held up.

4. *Light cruiser squadrons*

The cruiser squadron has the same organization as a light tank squadron, but is equipped with light cruisers instead of light tanks. A light cruiser is armed with an anti-tank Q.F. gun in addition to a light machine gun.

The role of the cruiser squadron is fighting ; to act in support of the light tank squadrons by attacking enemy opposition, particularly hostile tanks, which are holding up or otherwise preventing the light tank squadrons from carrying out their reconnaissance.

The cruiser squadron will thus usually be held in reserve in the hands of the regimental commander for employment as the situation requires.

In some circumstances, for instance in close difficult country or when the regiment is carrying out a delaying role, light cruiser troops may be allotted to work under the command of the light tank squadrons.

5. *Light tank troop*

A light tank troop consists of three light tanks.

The troop leader, who also commands his own tank, is in direct wireless communication with his squadron leader, and with all the other troops of his squadron. Although the other two tanks of the troop are also fitted with wireless sets, only the troop leader normally speaks on the wireless ; the sets in the other tanks are provided first of all to enable all tank commanders to listen-in to the messages and reports which pass between troop leaders and the squadron leader, and thus keep fully " in the picture," and, secondly, to provide a reserve of wireless should the troop leader's set break down.

The light tanks of the troop are wholly armoured against anti-tank small arms fire, and by reason of their small size are difficult targets to hit when in movement. *Movement* in combination with armour is the surest protection against becoming a casualty.

The light tank is armed with two weapons, a heavy machine gun for use against tanks, and a medium one for use against exposed personnel. It also carries a pair of projectors from which smoke candles can be fired to produce a smoke-screen to protect the tank from observation or fire. The projectors may, on occasions, be used also to throw a grapnel and line to tow away light obstacles which have been placed by the enemy to obstruct the tank's advance.

The armour, mobility and fire-power of the three tanks of a troop, put in the hands of the troop leader a unit with great powers of reconnaissance and considerable fighting value.

The primary task of the light tank troop is tactical reconnaissance, which means getting and transmitting the information about the enemy and the ground. This task implies fighting, when fighting is unavoidable, to obtain the required information ; or to defeat the enemy's reconnoitring troops and prevent them gaining information.

The detailed methods used by a troop in reconnaissance and fighting are dealt with later in this pamphlet. There is, however, one basic principle which covers them all—to make full use of armoured mobility, which is the distinctive characteristic of the tank.

Mobility, properly used, increases fighting power by adding surprise to fire-effect ; conversely, it answers enemy fighting power by minimising the effect of hostile anti-tank weapons. The aim must, therefore, always be to avoid immobility in the presence of the enemy, unless the troop is halted momentarily in a hull down or otherwise partly concealed position for the purpose of observing or engaging him by fire.

CHAPTER 1

THE ORGANIZATION AND TRAINING OF A LIGHT TANK CREW

2. Organization

The crew of a light tank consists of a commander, who is responsible for the tactical handling of the tank and for the administrative maintenance of the tank and its crew; a driver; and a gunner, who is also responsible for the wireless set which, however, is " operated " by the tank commander.

3. Objects

The object of crew training is to produce a team.

While each member of a crew must be master of his own particular function, all must be inter-changeable.

The purpose of crew training, therefore, is to ensure that every member :—

Is able to drive and maintain the tank.

Is master of the tank's weapons.

Is able to use (including tuning in) the wireless, and has a knowledge of signal codes.

Is a good map reader.

Is able to cook on the tank cooking set.

Has a knowledge of first-aid.

Has a working knowledge of the tactics of his own unit.

4. Driving

1. The driver must drive so as to :—

Make the fullest use of ground and cover to escape observation. Sky-lines must be avoided ; full advantage must be taken of shadows.

Assist the gunner to apply fire to the best advantage.

Achieve the most rapid and economical progress, saving petrol and avoiding unnecessary jolting to the crew and the machine.

Facilitate observation by the tank commander.

2. All the above must be achieved by the driver without constant orders and directions from the tank commander.

5. Gunnery

The gunner must be able to :—

Pick up targets quickly on brief orders. This can only be done if the gunner is constantly on the alert and anticipating targets by his own observation.

Make full use of favourable ground for the application of fire to the best advantage.

Apply self-imposed fire discipline to conserve ammunition and make full use of every round.

6. Wireless

It is the gunner's duty to look after the wireless set, to tune it in, and to prepare it for use by the tank commander.

Once the set is tuned in, the gunner should concentrate on manning his weapons and, except for periodic attention, leave the operating of the set to the tank commander.

7. Maintenance

The crew must be determined to keep their tank in action. Mechanical failure of a tank through an avoidable cause is a personal disgrace reflecting on every member of a crew. If their tank breaks down through accident the crew must spare no effort to repair it and re-join the troop. Calls by the crew for assistance from the unit fitters or R.A.O.C. should only be made reluctantly as the last resort in cases where repair is entirely beyond the resources of the crew.

Mechanical failures can only be avoided by thorough and continuous maintenance during periods of rest and at halts on the line of march. Every member must have his own definite responsibility so that every part of the tank and equipment is constantly inspected and attended to.

After a day's work no tank must be left by its crew until it is mechanically fit, re-fuelled and replenished and ready for action next day. Petrol and oil must be replenished at every opportunity during an operation.

Maintenance comes before rest.

CHAPTER 2

THE FORMATIONS AND MOVEMENT OF A TROOP

8. Troop formations

Troop formations are :—

Line ahead	The three tanks one behind the other.
Arrowhead	One tank leading, the other two following abreast.
Two-up	Two tanks abreast leading, the other following.
Line	The three tanks abreast.

9. Distances and intervals

No definite distances and intervals can be given in terms of yards as these will vary according to the ground and tactical conditions. Regular distances and intervals are to be avoided in all circumstances.

The following general rules must be applied :—

No tank should be out of sight of its troop leader for more than a few moments.

No tank should be beyond immediate support by at least one other tank of the troop.

The tanks of a troop should always be within control of the troop leader.

The tanks of a troop should never bunch so as to offer a single target to the enemy.

10. Speed

A high average speed is attained by judgment in the use of ground and by thinking ahead.

Never exceed the economical speed of the tank except in case of tactical necessity. Moving at speed for long periods results, eventually, in a broken-down tank through accident or mechanical failure.

But, never loiter.

11. Application of formations to ground and situation

1. The object of the troop leader is to adopt the formation which will best facilitate :—

Rapid movement.
Observation.
Protection against surprise.
Readiness for action.

He must be constantly weighing up which of these requirements is the most important in the situation in which he finds himself.

2. In choosing his formation the troop leader must bear in mind the following :—

- i. Maintenance of speed and direction is facilitated if tne troop leader leads his troop. *Line ahead* or *arrowhead*, with the troop leader leading, or *two-up* with the troop leader's tank as one of the forward tanks, will often, therefore, be the best formations to adopt during an approach march in conditions when the troop leader can see far enough ahead to be reasonably certain that surprise attack is unlikely.
- ii. *Line ahead*, although a useful and handy formation in close country or on roads, is obvious to air observation and is not a good fighting formation. It may also enable the enemy to shoot tanks one by one as they pass a gap or some exposed point. It should, therefore, only be adopted when the ground makes it unavoidable.
- iii. Once contact is gained the job of the troop leader is to place himself where he can best command and control his troop and where he can send back information. In these conditions, therefore, the most suitable formations are :—

   Line ahead, in the order point tank, troop leader, reserve tank.

   Arrowhead, with the troop leader's tank as one of the rear tanks.

   Two-up, with the troop leader's tank in rear.

- iv. *Two-up* enables the troop to observe a broad front. It is not an easy formation to handle when opposition is encountered because the troop leader has no reserve in hand except his own tank. This formation is seldom justified in close country owing to the danger of single tanks getting separated and out of support. Looping patrols (*i.e.* short detours round a wood or a side road) by a single tank may, on occasions, be justified.
- v. *Line* is primarily a fire formation adopted to enable the weapons of all three tanks to be brought to bear to the front. It is not a good formation for manœuvre although it should be adopted for crossing crests in open country.

vi. Tanks must avoid " tracking," *i.e.* blindly following the tank in front, on all occasions, even in *line ahead*.

Each tank must pick its own line and the troop should open out to *arrowhead* whenever the ground allows. On roads, alternate tanks should use opposite sides of the road.

This does not apply when tanks are moving into cover. Tanks must then follow the same track, if possible an existing one, since the track-marks of tanks are easily observed from the air.

12. Observation

1. *During movement*

To ensure that an all-round watch is maintained during movement, observation duties will be allocated within each crew and in the troop as follows :—

Within the crew.

Tank commander	all-round.
Gunner	near side.

In the troop.

i. In line ahead :—

Leading tank	..	front.
Second tank	..	near side.
Third tank	..	off side and rear.

ii. In other formations :—

All tanks will maintain all-round observation with weapons pointing in the direction of their own responsibility.

2. *Halting to observe*

When a troop halts to observe, full use will be made of all available cover. Particular care will be taken to obtain concealment by taking advantage of shadows, background, or folds in the ground if no actual cover is available. Tank commanders must appreciate the difference between a hull down position, when sufficient of the tank must be exposed to enable the weapons to be used, and a position of observation when the commander's head only needs to be in view.

Full use must be made of field glasses.

The troop should not close-up, or bunch ; once halted, tanks must keep still.

In some circumstances, as, for instance, in order to look over a high embankment which cannot be negotiated by the tank, it may be necessary for either the troop leader or a gunner to dismount to observe.

13. Use of ground

1. The tank is an extremely mobile vehicle in suitable conditions, but it is easily slowed down or stopped in unsuitable country. It is, therefore, of great importance that all ranks should be able to " use " ground to the best advantage.

The term " ground " includes formations such as hills, valleys, ridges and folds ; natural features such as woods and different types of cover. It also includes artificial features such as walls, buildings, ditches, hayricks, etc.

Every man must be able to appreciate the effect of these various features upon :—

> Observation.
> Concealment from view.
> Protection from fire.
> Fire positions.
> Movement.

2. *Observation*

Careful study of the map will generally give an indication of the best places from which observation can be obtained. Tank commanders and drivers must plan ahead and move from one selected position to the next, choosing the exact position at which they mean to halt as they approach. They must not think only in terms of high hills with long fields of view although, obviously, the farther they can see ahead and around them, the better. Covered approach and concealment from the enemy's view must also be considered.

3. *Concealment from view*

This can be obtained not only by getting into woods or behind hedges or buildings. Small folds, reverse slopes, shadows and background, often provide complete concealment for a stationary tank even in the open. Crest lines must be avoided by running along, turret down, just behind them.

4. *Protection from fire*

The ideal is to get hull down. This gives a large measure of protection from being hit and, further, the lack of background makes it difficult for the enemy gunner to observe and correct his fire.

5. *Fire positions*

Tank commanders and drivers must be able to recognise, instantly, positions from which fire can best be brought to bear on the enemy, and the most secure and quickest way to reach them. Other things being equal, it is an advantage to come into action on high ground to take advantage of the downhill running to change position or to close the range.

6. *Movement*

Commanders must avoid marshy ground, thick woods, narrow lanes with high banks, and very steep hills. Constant reference to the map seriously hinders observation. They must study the map beforehand and try to memorize it so that they have a good idea what the country is like which lies ahead and can anticipate, if they cannot avoid, difficulties. They must look ahead and think ahead and choose their line. It is often better, and quicker, to go a longer way round with a tank if the ground straight ahead looks doubtful.

14. March discipline

1. Strict march discipline is of the greatest importance to ensure that the maximum effort is obtained from men and machines. Under normal conditions, halts will be made as follows :—

> i. After the first 20 minutes marching, for 10 minutes. This halt is made to remedy any minor defects before they develop into serious faults.
> ii. Subsequently, after every 100 minutes marching, for 20 minutes.

These halts are essential for maintenance of machines and to rest the crews. They should be omitted only in cases of tactical emergency.

2. Every use must be made of cover during halts. If, when the order to halt is received, the troop has no cover available in the immediate vicinity, the troop leader should use his initiative and carry on until he reaches cover, if any is within easy reach.

3. The following points will be observed at halts. They will be applied at all times so that they become a drill.

> i. If on roads, tanks must pull clear of the road, and a traffic sentry must be posted.
> ii. Wireless watch will be kept, i.e., one man will remain in one tank to operate the wireless set.
> iii. Measures for local protection will be taken. This includes the detailing of a guard tank with its weapons manned and maintaining an all-round watch to guard against ground or air attack. When the squadron is marching as a whole, one guard tank per troop may not be necessary and guard tanks will be detailed under squadron arrangements.

iv. Tanks will never close up or bunch. It is better that one or two tanks should halt in the open rather than that the whole troop should be bunched in one small piece of cover.

v. Crews will proceed at once with maintenance, tank commanders reporting, on completion, their tank fit or otherwise, to the troop leader, who will in turn report to the squadron leader, if the squadron is marching as a whole.

vi. Casualties in personnel and tanks which have occurred since the last halt will be reported, and a collated report will be sent by the squadron leader to the regimental H.Q.

vii. If the squadron is marching as a column, troop leaders will report to the squadron leader as soon as possible, who will give them up-to-date information of the situation, mark their maps, and issue any necessary orders for the continuance of the march or operation. On return to their troops, troop leaders will similarly pass on all information, etc., to their tank commanders.

viii. After completion of their duties, crews will remain dismounted (unless otherwise ordered). Dismounted men must remain close to their tanks so as to be ready to mount quickly in case of alarm.

ix. Recognized alarm signals must be arranged.

15. Communications

1. *Means available*

The following means of inter-communication are available in the troop :—

Arm signals.	—Arm signal code.
Daylight signalling—	Arm signal code and tactical code sent by morse.
lamps.	
Wireless.	—Troop leader—squadron leader, two-way. (Other tanks normally listening : transmission only in emergency.)

In addition, in certain circumstances, scout cars may be allotted by regimental H.Q. to squadrons, and squadron leaders may sub-allot to troops.

2. *Wireless discipline*

Correct procedure must be observed.

Speakers must be sure of what they wish to say before switching on. If necessary, notes of map references and other details should be made beforehand.

Speakers must make sure that no one else is sending before beginning a conversation, or jamming may result.

Shouting and excited speech must be avoided.

The microphone must be kept close to the mouth.

Messages must be acknowledged promptly in the right order.

On conclusion of the conversation, the switch must be put back to " send."

Tuning calls must be kept to a minimum.

CHAPTER 3

TROOP TACTICS

16. General principles

1. Troop tactics are founded on the following broad principles. Training must aim at impressing these on every officer, n.c.o. and man of the troop.

i. *Mobility*

The outstanding characteristic of the tank is its armoured mobility. All tactics of armoured formations are based upon maintaining and exploiting this characteristic.

The action of the troop must, therefore, aim at :—

Avoiding frontal attacks.

Making full use of manœuvre (on the troop front), to find gaps and flanks.

Making the utmost use of speed to give protection and to fluster the defence.

In close country where manœuvre is restricted and speed is necessarily reduced, protection and mutual support assume the highest importance.

ii. *Teamwork*

The troop is a team and must be so trained that tank commanders and crews act intelligently on their own initiative for the benefit of the troop as a whole. Only by the development of a high degree of teamwork can the troop operate at speed without constant halts for the issue of verbal orders by its leader.

iii. *Surprise*

A surprised enemy is a half-beaten enemy. Skilful use of ground, quick thinking and speed in action are essential if surprise is to be achieved and the results fully exploited.

17. Reconnaissance tasks

1. *Forms of reconnaissance*

There are two main forms of reconnaissance task for the troop :—

i. The independent reconnaissance which is carried out at the order of the regimental or squadron commander, and is not governed by the task of the squadron from which the troop is temporarily detached.

ii. Reconnaissance carried out in co-operation with the other troops of the squadron under the orders of the squadron leader.

2. *Objects of reconnaissance*

i. The object of a troop in independent reconnaissance is to get the fullest possible information on a particular point or points defined by the commander who orders the reconnaissance. The troop therefore will have no other responsibilities, and will fight only when forced to do so in furtherance of its special mission.

ii. The objects of a troop reconnoitring as part of a squadron are more complex.

When the reconnaissance is primarily concerned with the enemy's armoured formations its objects will be not only to get information about the enemy's dispositions and movements, and about the ground, but also to prevent the enemy's patrols from getting similar information about our own troops.

Therefore, although the troop is chiefly concerned with locating formed bodies of the enemy, it should drive off the enemy's patrols whenever they are encountered.

If unable to do this, the troop leader should report to the squadron their location and direction of movement.

When the reconnaissance is primarily concerned with an immobile enemy, *e.g.*, a screen of infantry and anti-tank weapons, the troop should endeavour to locate the enemy's dispositions in general and, having reported them, should seek to pass through gaps or round flanks in order to continue the reconnaissance for the hostile main bodies.

3. *Frontage*

A light armoured regiment employed on reconnaissance moves on a broad front, usually with its two light tank squadrons deployed, and its cruiser squadron in reserve. A light tank squadron, similarly, moves with two or three troops up, according to the ground.

To lay down the approximate frontage to be covered by any unit or formation however small is difficult and liable to lead to too rigid application since the governing factors are always the task in hand, the ground and the anticipated action of the enemy.

Where the task for a troop involves detailed reconnaissance of the ground either to discover the dispositions of troops who may be in position, or for routes over obstacles, etc., it may be taken that in ordinary open country in Western Europe a troop can cover 1,000 yards or so. In close country where movement is restricted to roads and tracks, the frontage taken up will depend upon the number of routes available ; one troop normally being allotted one road.

In very open country such as might be met with in the Middle East, visibility may allow of a troop being allotted a much greater frontage. Where this is the case it does not mean that the tanks of a troop are distributed over that area, for at all times the tanks of a troop must be within mutually supporting distance.

4. *Control*

Control and direction are maintained by the use of :—

 i. Bounds.
 ii. Centre lines.

5. *Bounds*

Successive " bounds " will be defined by the squadron leader, on reaching which, troop leaders will send back their reports. These bounds, which will usually be well-defined features such as a road, railway or river line, will not necessarily coincide with tactical objectives. Providing wireless is in use there will be no need for troops to halt on these bounds for purposes of control.

If the ground lying between bounds is such as to make it necessary, the troop leader may lay down his own intermediate bounds, at which he will get a signal from his leading tank or tanks.

Should wireless silence be imposed by order or by breakdown, the old system of movement will be adopted, and the troop, on reaching the bound laid down by the squadron leader, will halt, report, and await orders before moving on.

6. *Centre lines*

Each regiment and squadron will be given a centre line, along which its headquarters will move. Centre lines are ordered for the purposes of maintaining direction, and controlling the movement of headquarters so that they can readily be found by liaison officers, scout cars, etc., carrying written or verbal reports and messages.

Troop centre lines are not required. The troop leader, who will know his squadron centre line and whether he is right, centre or left troop, is able to maintain direction in relation to the squadron centre line and by periodic visual touch with troops on his flanks. He is in sight of his other two tanks. Thus, if he is leading his troop the other tanks will conform to his movements; if he is not leading, the troop leader will direct his other tanks, who must " keep their eyes " on him, by signal. Rallying the tanks of a troop to give them verbal directions may occasionally be necessary. It is liable to be dangerous, and with a well-trained troop should be rare.

7. *Dividing lines*

Dividing lines between troops are not required, as troops are in intermittent visual touch and will be aware of the position of troops on their flanks by overhearing their reports and messages.

The laying down of dividing lines increases the time taken in issuing and assimilating orders, and is only necessary when it is essential to define accurately the responsibility of regiments and squadrons for covering ground.

8. *Orders*

Before an operation every troop leader will receive orders and instructions. These will vary for each operation but should always include :—

i. Information—about the enemy—and about our own troops.

ii. The superior commander's intention, which should contain the object of the operation as a whole as well as the intention of the squadron leader. It is most important that a troop leader should fully understand the underlying intention so that in a situation which may change rapidly, he shall be able to co-operate intelligently with any neighbouring troops for the execution of the general plan.

iii. The method by which the operation will be carried out. This usually covers the tasks allotted to the squadron to which the troop leader belongs as well as those allotted to his troop. Also centre lines (regimental and squadron)—and any other particular points governing the way in which the task is to be carried out.

Where not already provided for, administrative and signal orders will have to be included.

The troop leader will give his own orders and instructions to his tank commanders. It is upon the completeness of these orders and instructions that the success or failure of the troop and the speed and flexibility of mobile armoured operations depend.

During an operation all troop leaders and tank commanders can and must continuously listen-in to the reports of the other troop leaders in their squadron ; furthermore, troop leaders must take every opportunity at halts, when rallied, etc., to ensure that their tank commanders are fully in possession of the latest information. (*See* Chapter 2, sec. **14,** para. 3, vii.)

9. *Reports*

    i. *First contact*

First contact with the enemy must always be reported as soon as possible unless the squadron leader is so placed that he is aware of it at the moment when it is made.

    ii. *Location reports*

These are only required at the places and times laid down by the squadron leader, *i.e.*, on bounds. Constant and indiscriminate giving of location reports prejudices secrecy unnecessarily and is a mis-use of the wireless.

    iii. *Reconnaissance reports*

These must be brief and clear. This takes much practice. Differentiate between facts and deduction. If sent by wireless, they must always be sent personally by the troop leader. If sent by written message, observe the correct procedure, abbreviations, etc., as given in F.S.P.B., Pamphlet No. 2, 1939, Appendix II.

    iv. *Getting back information*

Neighbouring troops must assist by relaying other troops' messages if it is apparent that messages are not being received by the squadron leader.

If the troop leader's wireless is out of action, he should trans-ship into one of the other tanks of his troop.

If all wireless communication is impossible the troop leader *must get any important information back* and, in the last resort, must send back one of his tanks with a written or verbal message either to a neighbouring troop or to squadron H.Q.

It may often be necessary to send back a tank as a guide when it is required to bring the squadron leader to a point which cannot (or must not) be accurately described on the wireless.

18. Action on encountering hostile anti-tank defence in open country.

1. *Immediate action*

Leading tank drops smoke candles and manœuvres out of immediate danger. It is better, if ground allows, to speed up and run diagonally under cover of own smoke than to attempt to turn away sharply.

Following tanks open out to get the hostile anti-tank gun looking in two directions and confuse his aim, and to bring converging fire to bear on suspected locality.

On no account must tanks halt in the open. To so do plays into the hands of the defence. If no other course is open, it is best to speed up and jink. Speed is the best protection and rapid action may well fluster the enemy gunner.

2. *Subsequent action*

Opposition should be avoided if possible, but anti-tank guns are seldom sited singly, and if they are mutually supporting, an attempt to manœuvre may lead the troop into further difficulties. In these circumstances it may be better to attack.

If attack is decided upon, the troop leader should aim at " pinning " the located enemy by fire with the leading tank from a concealed or hull down position, while the remaining two tanks manœuvre round the flank and attack and destroy the enemy from the flank or rear.

It is sounder to " pin " with one tank and to manœuvre with the remaining two than to " pin " with two and attempt to manœuvre with a single tank. During the movement round the flank the two tanks will generally need to afford each other mutual support against other opposition. A single tank would be at a disadvantage in this respect.

For similar reasons, and because of the difficulty of control, it is seldom a sound procedure for a troop to adopt the " pincer " tactics, *i.e.*, attempt to send single tanks simultaneously round both flanks.

19. Action on encountering a defended river line

1. Attack on a defended river crossing will seldom be a feasible operation by a light tank troop without support.

The object of the troop will be, therefore, to find an undefended crossing and, if the selected crossing is held, to reconnoitre thoroughly all possible crossings on its front.

Main crossings are usually approached through defiles, villages, etc. If opposition is known or strongly suspected, it will usually be advisable for the troop to avoid the main crossing and attempt first to cross at some minor crossing which appears from the map to exist on its front.

2. If an undefended crossing is found, the troop should cross and report immediately.

The subsequent action of the troop will depend upon the task on which it is engaged and on the instructions it has been given by the squadron leader.

It may take up a position to secure the crossing ; or continue its advance ; or open neighbouring crossings by attacking the defenders in rear (this usually would be a task undertaken by reserve troops or even the reserve squadron).

3. If unable to cross anywhere on the troop front, the troop commander should inform his squadron commander of the locality which appears most suitable for attack, and should dispose his troop so as to be ready to give support should it be decided that such an attack is to be made.

For forcing a crossing the plan should provide for covering fire as in any other tactical operation.

Such a plan might be for the light tank troops in the vicinity to co-operate to bring the maximum fire to bear to support the attack by the reserve light tank troops, or by the cruiser squadron.

On the attacking troops getting over, these light tank troops would follow and pass through them, either to enlarge the bridge-head by seizing commanding ground on the far bank, or to continue their tasks.

4. It should not be overlooked that it may be practicable to cross at other places than at recognized crossing places. The troop leader should not, therefore, be satisfied with merely reconnoitring bridges and marked fords only. If these are all held a careful reconnaissance of the entire river bank in his sector must be made. This is one of the occasions when a dismounted reconnaissance may be necessary.

20. Action on encountering a defended railway

The same procedure applies as in the case of a water obstacle. Few railways, however, present continuous obstacles. Main bridges and tunnels should be avoided, and attempts should be made to effect a crossing on level ground or where cuttings and embankments meet.

21. Method of movement on roads when opposition expected

Protection assumes great importance. The order of march —point tank, troop leader, reserve—should, therefore, be adopted.

Tanks should always be in sight of each other and able to give mutual support.

Movement, therefore, takes the form of a series of bounds from one bend or crest to the next.

Full distances should be maintained between tanks on the straight or level stretches.

On approaching a bend (or crest), the point tank slows down or halts momentarily, where it can see round, keeping well into one side or other.

The following tanks speed up and reduce distances so as to be ready to support quickly.

If all is clear, the troop proceeds, opening out again to full distances if the road is straight or level round the corner or over the crest.

22. Method of movement through a hostile village street

Close down.

The leading tank should move close into left of the road watching its front and ready to fire at windows of houses on the right side ; the following tank should move close into the right of the road ready to fire at windows on the left side ; the rear tank should move on the left of the road and cover the rear.

Distances between tanks are governed to some extent by the height of the houses ; the taller the houses, the greater the distances required to allow the guns to be brought to bear.

Full protected movement must be adopted as in sec. 21

Move quickly over cross-roads and road junctions, and swing guns ready to fire down them.

Avoid halting.

23. Action on encountering a defended road block

1. *Immediate action*

On encountering a road block the leading tank must never halt. This is what the defenders hope he will do as it gives them a sitting shot. It must take cover immediately (using its smoke candles if necessary to protect its movement) and signal the following tanks to halt.

2. *Reconnaissance*

Reconnaissance should then be made from cover by the leading tank or troop leader, dismounted if necessary, to discover the nature of the obstacle, the location of defending weapons, and possible ways round without attacking.

3. *Plan*

If reconnaissance has shown that there is no way of getting on except by attack on the obstacle, the troop leader should report this to the squadron leader before carrying on. An attack on a road block may be expensive in casualties because of the lack of manœuvre room ; on the other hand, a gap may have been discovered by another troop elsewhere on the squadron front. In such circumstances, it is for the squadron leader to decide whether the troop should attack or remain in observation pending developments elsewhere. When it is decided to make an attack, where there is no way round, it may be possible to remove the obstacle by towing if it is not very strongly constructed or defended. The troop leader's plan would embody the use of grapnel ; covering fire, including smoke ; and an advance through the gap.

4. If there is no way round and the obstacle cannot be dealt with, the troop should remain in observation.

24. Action on encountering a minefield

The same general procedure applies as in the case of a defended road block, except that no means exist with light tank troops for removing mines. The only way to remove them is by dismounted men.

It must be anticipated that the presence of a minefield will usually only be discovered by the fact that the leading tank has been disabled.

The only practicable method of dealing with such opposition is, therefore, by a squadron plan involving the employment of the reserve troop or troops.

The action of a leading troop should be to report ; to look for a way round, and, if penetration of the minefield is decided upon by the squadron commander, remain in observation and adopt dispositions to support the subsequent action.

25. Action on encountering hostile tanks

1. Information that tanks have been met is of vital importance. Their location, number, type and direction of movement must be reported at once.

2. If the enemy force consists of light tanks in small numbers the troop should avoid being drawn away from its task. It should carry on unless ordered otherwise by squadron leader. The troop job is to get on and get through the enemy's reconnaissance troops, and to discover and report the main bodies behind.

3. If enemy tanks are in strength and consist of heavy tanks which are likely to attack or interfere with the squadron or regiment in the execution of its task, they cannot be ignored. In this case the troop may be ordered by the squadron leader to co-operate in the subsequent cruiser squadron action.

In default of orders, the troop should keep the enemy tanks under observation.

4. If the cruiser squadron is employed, the action of the light tank troop will be on the following lines :—

    i. Piquet the enemy and keep the squadron leader fully informed of movements and developments. Engage enemy reconnaissance elements, which attempt to advance and gain information of the movements of the cruiser squadron. In other words, gain all the information possible, and prevent the enemy from gaining it.

    ii. If threatened or attacked by superior numbers, or heavy tanks, the troop must manœuvre. It cannot take them on, but it can delay and hamper them by short bursts of fire, causing them to close down, and can divert their attention and possibly draw them on to unfavourable ground, thus creating an opportunity for decisive action by the cruiser squadron.

    iii. Avoid a running fight. Tank combats are won by fire. Greater accuracy is attained from a stationary tank. The troop leader's object must be, therefore, to deploy his tanks so that they can bring fire to bear from stationary, concealed positions. This entails skilful use of ground and rapid movement between selected positions.

26. Action of a troop in defence

1. A regiment or a squadron may, on occasions, be employed in a defensive role, such as denying an area to the enemy. The method employed will be for a proportion of the light tank troops to take up positions on likely lines of enemy advance while the remaining troops and squadrons are held concentrated ready to counter-attack any enemy that penetrate into the area.

2. The following points deal with the dispositions and action of a light tank troop :—

    i. The object is achieved by surprise fire, therefore, concealment is essential. Careful selection of positions must be made, taking advantage of natural cover and background. Individual tank commanders must be capable of siting their own tanks. Alternative positions must be reconnoitred.

    ii. Good fields of observation are desirable. Extensive observation to enable opening of long-range fire is not essential. Greater effect and economy of ammunition is obtained by opening fire at medium range.

iii. The extent of dispersion of the troop is governed by the means of control available in the troop. Tanks must usually, therefore, be within sight of (and signal by) the troop leader.

iv. Isolated cover should be avoided. It is often better to be hull down in open.

v. If the troop is likely to be in its position for long, rest and relief must be organized. It may be possible to arrange for one tank at a time to be " on guard." Personnel must be relieved on a roster. If relief by tanks is not practicable owing to the danger of giving away the position, all personnel must be pooled, and relief arranged by crews.

vi. The guard tank must have its crew on duty, with gun manned and loaded; commander in the turret; driver in his seat.

Men resting may, if the situation permits, dismount but remain close to tanks.

3. Occasionally tank units may be required to hold ground in co-operation with infantry from the divisional support group, or some other formation.

When this is done the troops in each sector (troop, squadron or regimental) will be under one command so that the tasks of the tanks and the infantry may be properly co-ordinated. As a general guide the tanks will be employed for reconnaissance and as a mobile reserve and the infantry will provide the garrisons of the defended localities.

4. If a troop is likely to be employed for counter-attack, the ground and probable routes over which counter-attacks may have to be made should be thoroughly reconnoitred beforehand.

5. Tanks by themselves are not suitable for holding ground by night, and normally they should be withdrawn behind the protection of other troops for rest and maintenance.

Should it be necessary, in exceptional circumstances, to leave them to assist infantry in holding by night the ground which they have occupied by day as in para. 3, above, the roles will be reversed and the infantry will take over the duties of reconnaissance and protection and the tanks will be placed so that they can support the action of the infantry with the fire of their machine guns.

6. Light tanks may be used in withdrawal actions and, on account of their mobility, are well suited to be left to be the last troops to disengage from the enemy.

When the time comes to move there must be no delay. Tanks must be facing exits from cover with the route of withdrawal reconnoitred. All tank commanders must be given definite instructions as to the withdrawal signal and the action to be taken.

A troop may have difficulty in remaining in its original position, once the position has been disclosed. Therefore, previous reconnaissance of a rearward position must be made if time permits. The allotment of a scout car to the troop will be of great value in carrying out such reconnaissance. If this is not possible, the troop leader must have a clear-cut plan for withdrawal by known routes, to a previously arranged rendezvous.

27. Action when attacked by hostile aircraft

1. Every precaution must be taken to avoid observation by enemy aircraft. By this means the chances of being attacked can be greatly minimised.

2. Concealment from air observation can be achieved by :—

   i. The adoption of irregular formations. Regular distances and intervals between tanks, whether on roads or when moving across country must, therefore, be avoided.

   ii. The use of natural cover. *E.g.* the troop should run on the shady side of the road.

   iii. If halted, advantage must be taken of all available cover, including camouflage equipment, grass, branches, etc.

   iv. If halted for long periods as, for example, in bivouac, track marks made when driving *into* cover must be obliterated. Movement must be avoided and, by night, the exposure of lights.

3. If attacked when on the move the troop will :—

   i. Close down.

   ii. If on a road, turn off into open formation. If it is impossible to leave the road the most open formation possible must be maintained.

   iii. If in the open, adopt the widest extension possible and jink to avoid diving attacks.

   iv. Uncontrolled speeding up gives no protection and increases the danger of collision if a tank is hit. Speed should be increased only to quicken dispersion—when this has been achieved normal speed and control must be resumed.

4. Normally when a troop is halted it should be so dispersed, whether under cover or in the open, as to offer a poor target to aircraft even if discovered.

If attacked when halted the troop will :—

  i. Close down.
  ii. If under cover, remain concealed.
  iii. If discovered insufficiently dispersed, whether under cover or in the open, disperse more widely.

28. Protection at rest

Tank units will normally go into bivouac in areas which are protected by other troops from the risk of ground attack. No area, however, can be considered as absolutely safe in this respect, and tank units, like other troops, are at all times responsible for their own protection.

By night, whenever possible, infantry from the divisional support group will be allotted to tank units for local protection, but this does not absolve the tanks themselves from adopting tactically sound dispositions, or the crews from being ready to man their vehicles and weapons at short notice.

If for any reason infantry are not available for the local protection of bivouacs, dismounted sentry groups will be posted on all approaches at such a distance from the bivouac as will enable warning of enemy action to be given, so that crews may man their vehicles and weapons.

Often spare crews will be present in bivouac areas by night, and will provide additional personnel for outpost duty if necessary.

CHAPTER 4

POINTS OF PROCEDURE IN TROOP ACTION

29. Hull down action

Object. To enable a tank or troop to engage the enemy while, at the same time, presenting the smallest possible target to the enemy.

Troop leaders and tank commanders must learn to make utmost use of ground for this purpose.

Besides spurs and well defined ridges, quite small folds of the ground, if used skilfully, provide the necessary cover.

Drivers must be trained to place their tanks hull down accurately and quickly, without orders or directions from the tank commander.

Much practice is required.

A recognized drill for occupation of a hull down position should be developed in the troop.

The troop should first form in line well below the crest, then advance in line to its position. Thus the simultaneous opening of fire (giving surprise and maximum fire effect) will be possible, and the enemy will be unable to concentrate his fire, as would be possible if tanks were to appear singly at intervals.

This drill must be practised so that it can be carried out quickly and accurately. Troops will then be able to manœuvre quickly from one fire position to another. By this means, fire can be brought to bear from varying directions ; the enemy's fire will be dispersed, and the enemy will be confused as to the strength of the attack.

Withdrawal from a hull-down position can often best be carried out by tanks reversing initially until below the crest.

Wireless aerials should be pulled down to avoid these prematurely giving away the position.

30. Employment of smoke projectors

Characteristics—limited range ; limited ammunition ; inaccurate ; outside loading.

While smoke produced from light tank projectors is primarily intended for the immediate protection of the individual tank, *e.g.*, when suddenly fired on by anti-tank gun, it may on occasions be used collectively by a troop as far as its characteristics allow. The limited number of candles carried entails strict fire discipline.

Quick decision and judgment are required. Candles should be dropped up-wind between the tank and enemy. If there is room to manœuvre the tank should run down wind to take full advantage of the smoke. The maximum screen develops at some distance from the candle itself. Subsequently, the screen may have to be thickened or prolonged with subsequent shots.

Both projectors should always be kept loaded.

31. Use of single tanks

The troop is a team which relies on mutual cc-operation and support between tanks; a single tank is extremely vulnerable.

In principle, any manœuvre which entails the movement or action of a single tank out of support of its fellows, is unsound.

The use of single tanks may, of course, be justified in certain circumstances, *e.g.*, message carrying in emergency; limited looping patrols; or in the event of the troop being reduced to two tanks by casualty.

32. Closing down

It is necessary to balance protection against observation, speed, and comfort.

Speed is necessarily reduced when closed down.

Long, or frequent, periods of closed running seriously affect the endurance of the crew. As a general rule tanks travel opened-up (commander's cupola and driver's flap open).

When action is impending the driver's flap must be closed. The commander's and gunner's flaps should also be closed when the tank is subjected to close range accurate fire and when bombing or fire is likely to be brought to bear from above.

33. Dismounting

1. Men should not be dismounted except for good reasons.

By dismounting, personnel are deprived of the protection of the armour, of the use of the tank weapons, and of means of communication.

Personnel should *never* be outside their tanks when there is a chance of the tank becoming engaged with the enemy.

At recognized halts for rest and maintenance, crews may be dismounted, but full protective precautions must be taken.

2. Single men may be dismounted, provided they remain within sight and reach of their tanks, for specific reasons, of which the following are examples :—

  i. To look over a high obstacle, such as a railway embankment, or round thick cover, when adequate observation cannot be obtained from the tank itself.

  ii. To examine a river bank with a view to crossing at an unmarked crossing.

iii. To remove mines or a road block if these are not covered by the enemy.

34. Action by crew of a disabled tank

1. If the tank can be repaired by the crew it should be moved to the nearest cover, if it is movable, and the repair completed. The gun must be manned.

After repair, the tank should carry on with its task or, if some time has elapsed, follow on the squadron or regimental centre line as last known.

2. If the tank cannot be repaired by the crew the commander will :—

   i. Report position by wireless, stating nature of casualty, and assistance, particularly spare parts, required.
   He should *not* ask for assistance until he is sure that the fault cannot be remedied by the crew.

   ii. If the tank is movable, it should be moved to the nearest cover which facilitates concealment and protection.

   iii. Gun and wireless should be manned continuously.

   iv. If forced to abandon a tank, which is liable to fall into enemy hands, weapons and mechanism should be rendered useless, if circumstances permit, by removing locks, breech blocks, etc., and burring edges of working parts. The tank should be set on fire. (*See* note at bottom of page.)
   All papers, codes, maps, etc., and all means of identification should be removed or destroyed. The crew should then move on foot towards unit centre line.

   v. Except in circumstances of extreme tactical emergency, any tank passing near a disabled tank should halt momentarily to give any immediate assistance possible, and to ascertain the nature of the breakdown, etc. This information should be reported as soon as possible to squadron H.Q.

NOTE.—As the petrol tank is armour-protected, it is difficult to cause a fire by puncturing the petrol tank. Probably the best way to start a fire is to break a petrol lead and let some petrol run out and set this free petrol alight by a match or by firing a Verey light.

35. Dealing with a wounded man

1. Apply first-aid.

2. Report the casualty to squadron H.Q. at the first opportunity.

3. If the wound is not serious, it is best to carry the casualty in the tank until the squadron rallies.

4. If the man is seriously hurt, and impedes the remainder of crew badly, he should be taken out of the tank at the first opportunity, and made as comfortable as possible under cover. It will greatly increase the chances of medical attention and collection if casualties are placed on the squadron or, if possible, brigade centre line. The exact location of the place where the man is placed should be carefully noted, and reported at first opportunity. Do not forget to leave water, food, and a blanket or coat with the casualty.

36. Treatment of prisoners and action on being taken prisoner

1. It is normally uneconomical to use tanks as escorts to prisoners.

Small bodies of the enemy who surrender will generally have to be left. They must be disarmed and evidence of identification (badges, buttons and papers) taken from them.

Weapons must be rendered useless by the removal of bolts and other vital parts or destroyed by running over them.

Large bodies of enemy who surrender should, if possible, be reported to squadron H.Q., and kept under observation pending orders by the squadron leader. Escorts may be found by light tank troops or from the support group.

2. *See* F.S.P.B., Pamphlet No. 3, 1939, Sec. 17, for action on being taken prisoner.

37. Rallying

Between phases of an operation, squadrons may be ordered to rally for the purpose of allowing the squadron leader to issue fresh orders for a new phase ; or of giving crews the opportunity for rest and maintenance or, possibly, at the end of an approach march, to re-fill.

Rallying does *not* mean forming up in parade formations in close order. Troops and tanks will be within call, but scattered under available cover. If no cover available, every advantage must be taken of dead ground, and the adoption of irregular dispersed formations becomes even more important.

Immediately on reaching the rallying position, troop leaders will report to the squadron leader, while the remainder of crews carry on with maintenance.

Crews will not fall out for a rest until maintenance is completed.

Full protective measures will always be taken.

CHAPTER 5

ANTI-GAS

38. Notes on tanks and blister gas

1. The effect on tanks passing over ground heavily contaminated with liquid blister gas.

Mustard vapour. Will enter the tank, and respirators must be put on when tanks are in a gas-contaminated area. The vapour will leave the tank fairly soon after the tank has left the contaminated area.

It is unlikely that the skin of men within the tank will be affected unless the tank remains in the contaminated area for a considerable period, *e.g.* on a very hot day 30 to 45 minutes, depending on whether the area is heavily contaminated or not. The vapour given off from mustard and mud on the track will not be strong enough to affect the skin.

Liquid mustard. The tracks and undercarriage, especially on very muddy ground, will get covered with earth containing liquid mustard.

It is unlikely that the tank, even when passing over very muddy ground, will get contaminated above the mudguards.

2. The decontamination of tanks passing over a contaminated area.

As soon as possible after leaving the contaminated area, tanks should be run over clean land or through water, and should make a number of quick turns, after which as much mud as possible should be scraped off the tracks. The process should be repeated as opportunity offers.

Tanks should be kept in the open, and not in closed sheds, for a week after passing through a contaminated area, so as to avoid any risk of vapour affecting men in the sheds. As an additional precaution, men repairing the tracks for a month afterwards should wear anti-gas gloves, or if the work is not of more than 10 minutes duration and the wearing of gloves interferes with its execution, hands may be rubbed with ointment which should be removed immediately on completion of the work.

One method of ensuring that the tracks are completely free from mustard is by hosing with water and " picking " off the earth, after which the tracks should be removed and decontaminated with petrol and cotton waste swabs.

3. In the event of an attack by aircraft using spray on a column of tanks on the march, tanks should be closed down when the attack takes place. If the cover of the turret is open and spray enters, not only will the crew get contaminated, but the interior of the tank also.

The crevices, corners and machinery will be difficult to decontaminate. When the tanks are moving with their turrets open, sentries must keep a sharp look-out for hostile aircraft.

4. If after a spray attack tanks are contaminated with drops of liquid mustard, the whole of the outside will probably not require decontamination. The main consideration is to decontaminate with petrol and cotton waste swabs, the doors or places where men enter and leave the tank. When it is necessary to leave the tank, one man must decontaminate the exit with petrol and cotton waste. He can then carefully get out and swab all round the door, step, etc., of the exit.

If time permits, as much as possible (less muddy tracks) of the exterior of the tank may be cleansed with petrol and swabs. The swabs must be burnt after use as they will contain mustard as well as petrol.

5. Precaution against aircraft spray when tanks are in bivouac. (*See also* Protection against Gas and Air Raids Pamphlet No. 1, 1930, Sec. 49, 3.)

    i. All sentries must watch gas-spray detectors, which should be placed on the ground and vehicles.

    ii. Crews should sleep under tarpaulins or ground sheets, and as close to their tanks as possible.

    iii. Some petrol, bleach powder and cotton waste should be placed outside the tank and covered over.

    iv Tanks should be closed down to prevent spray entering.

    v. If the tactical situation permits, crews should stay under cover of bivouacs until morning. A thorough reconnaissance can then be carried out.

    vi. When the warning is given to enter tanks, the doors and entrances should be decontaminated with petrol. A heap of bleach should be placed on the ground near the door. Each man of the crew will step on the bleach before entering the tank, and rub boots *well* in the bleach.

    vii. The tarpaulin should be carefully rolled up by men wearing anti-gas gloves, or, failing these, anti-gas ointment should be applied to the hands before and after the removal of the tarpaulin.

        For some days the tarpaulin should be marked as " contaminated " and should be handled only by men wearing anti-gas gloves, etc. Tarpaulins must be unrolled as soon as possible and be allowed to weather.

Printed under the Authority of HIS MAJESTY'S STATIONERY OFFICE by William Clowes & Sons, Ltd., London and Beccles.

TRAINING MANUALS, TEXT BOOKS AND INSTRUCTIONS

The backbone of all successful armies is its training and tactics. The Naval and Military Press publishes many such manuals of instruction – all perviously long out of print . So, whether your interest lies in the infantry and cavalry tactics of the earliest regiments of the British army in the 18th century, or the weapons manuals and firing instructions of 20th century warfare, the Naval and Military Press has the right book for you.

www.naval-military-press.com

MINES AND BOOBY TRAPS 1943

This is a War Office pamphlet, issued mid-war, in 1943. Its purpose is to introduce sappers to mines commonly used by the British Army – and how to deal with similar devices set by the Germans. The devices described and illustrated cover British anti-tank; grenade; shrapnel and assorted booby trap switches. Enemy mines are covered in chapter 2 with anti-tank, Teller mine types; French anti-tank; Hungarian; anti-personnel German and Italian; and igniters.This is a concise but comprehensive guide for British Army sappers in the art of demining or mine clearance.
9781474539395

THE .303 LEWIS GUN

Illustrated with good clear line drawings this 1941 weapon guide tells the Home Guard Volunteer how to use the 303 Lewis Gun effectively against the invading enemy.A reprint of an original handbook for the .303 Lewis Gun, that was first published in 1941. This book is a practical guide to the handling and maintenance of this iconic weapon.In the crisis following the Fall of France, where a large part of the British Army's equipment had been lost up to and at Dunkirk, stocks of Lewis guns in both .303 and .30-06 were hurriedly pressed back into service, primarily for Home Guard use. Full of fascinating information, this book taught the user the guns capabilities and all he needed to know about maintenance and combat use. Number 2 in the wartime Nicholson & Watson "Know Your Weapons" series, that offer all the important information in a more vivid style than an official publication. Illustrated with good clear line drawings.
9781474539456

ANTI-TANK WEAPONS
Smash The Tank

An insight into the amateur side of World War 2. Diagrams illustrate the main points and the devices, such as the Thermos Bomb;Phosrhorus Bomb;Sticky Bombs; that could be cobbled together from household items are described.This pamphlet was available to the Home Guard and describes the German tank and how to destroy it. It is an early War publication c1940, dealing with the light tanks used by the Germans, also the author gives examples of anti-tank actions in the Spanish Civil War, in which he took part. I'ts is a fascinating look at the "enthusiastic" approach to killing tanks.

9781474539449

TANK HUNTING AND DESTRUCTION 1940

The stated object for the distributing of this War Office manual was as "A guide and help to troops who have the determination and nerve to destroy tanks at close quarters". Intended for fighting on home soil after the very real possibility of a full German invasion, "Operation Sea Lion", this is a remarkable if somewhat naive snap shot of Britain state of preparedness,in her most dangerous hour.

The contents details Tank hunting, Tank characteristics,Tactical action,Road blocks,ambushes Ect,also includes an interesting appendix on Molotov Cocktails, and materials on other ways to destroy tanks.

9781474539401

TROOP TRAINING FOR LIGHT TANK TROOPS NOVEMBER 1939

Very early War tactics pertaining to various aspects of training with and employing armour in the British Army. Covering in concise detail that which a Light tank crew needed to know to be effective in action. In the early years of the war, Germany held the initiative. German forces used Blitzkrieg tactics in France in 1940, making full use of the speed and armour of tanks to break through enemy defences. It was clear that German tank tactics had evolved during the inter-war period. By contrast, Britain and the Allies were playing catch-up.

9781474539302

JAPANESE WEAPONS ILLUSTRATED
September 1944

This period 'Restricted' laced binding manual was intended to be an aid to the identification of Japanese Army equipment, with sections covering: Tanks, both two-man, Tankette, light and medium; Armoured Cars; Self-Propelled Guns; Anti-Tank Guns; Artillery; Anti-Aircraft Guns; Mortars & Grenade Dischargers; Small Arms; Flamethrowers etc. Produced one year before the surrender of Japan, this work gives a good overview of the weapons the allies would find, fighting an army that despite being on the back foot, was still capable of stiff resistance in an almost entirely defensive role..

9781474539432

NOTES ON THE GERMAN ARMY-WAR
December 1940

An early war 393-page 'Notes' periodical manual from December 1940. It is a detailed review, for use in the field. The manual looks at every aspect of the "Blitzkrieg" German Army (and, to some extent, the Air Force) and gives details as known at the time.

It covers the fighting arms and the services behind them – tactics, organisation, weapons and equipment. It usefully also includes a colour section on uniforms and insignia, a black-and-white plate section of small arms, infantry support and anti-tank weapons, artillery and AFVs. A series of pull-outs related to the text covering tanks etc. are also reproduced.

This is an important first-class picture of the complex fighting machine that was the German Army at the end of the campaigns of 1940, only six months before the invasion of Russia.

9781474539203

GERMAN MINES AND TRAPS

Mid-1940 War Office manual with details of German mines, both the Teller and S-mine (Bouncing Betty) are covered, with techniques for disarming. Good clear full-page line drawings give both practical and technical information. Highly recommended because of the illustrations, which show how these devices worked and the components.

9781474535809

NOTES ON ENEMY ARMY IDENTIFICATIONS ITALY
October 1941

This period handbook was published to give British military personnel a better understanding of the principal characteristics of both the Italian army and the Black Shirt Militia under active service conditions , it is dated October 1941.

It begins with a description of distinctive branches, or specialities, the most characteristic of which was the arm of the Royal Carabinieri, a semi-military body occupying, historically, the senior position in the Army. Other specialities included the Grenadiers of Sardinia, the Bersaglieri, the Alpini and the San Marco Marine Regiment

The handbook then goes on to show, in order, the organisation of Command and Staff, of formations (corps and divisions) and of the arms and services; services, supply and transportation; ranks, plates (many in colour) cover uniforms, insignia, medals and decorations; armament and equipment and a chapter on the Air Force, There are chapters on tactical doctrine and principles of employment, on permanent fortifications, camouflage and abbreviations. Finally there is a brief index.

9781474539746

MANUAL OF GUERILLA TACTICS
Specially Prepared And Based On Lessons From
The Spanish And Russian Campaigns

One of the excellent, concise Bernards Pocket Books, intended to show members of the Home Guard and the regular forces that war is not conducted in a gentlemanly way – it is kill or be killed.

9781474539463

THE OFFENSIVE OF SMALL UNITS
September 1916

This is a periodical tactical manual from 1916, it focuses on the manner in which the French organised and executed their attacks and counterattacks . Summarised from the French, it lays out the process by which to operate in attacks on the German trenches. Focused purely on the operation of infantry, the purpose of this British translation is to give small infantry units the benefit of the French experience in regard to the best methods of combat, in offensive operations.

9781474537971

TRENCH WARFARE
Notes on attack and defence, February 1915

This important period manual was published in early 1915 when hope of a quick ending to the war disappeared, and trench warfare had begun to dominate the Western Front.

The manual strives to instil an offensive spirit and gives practical examples on: Close quarter, local, methods of successful warfare, and German attacks. The salient points to gather were preparation and co-operation between artillery and infantry, and that the capture of trenches is easier than their retention. Two plates illustrating tactics complete this official publication.

9781474539807

Ministry Of Home Security
OBJECTS DROPPED FROM THE AIR 1941

An illustrated Official and confidential publication, covering the many and varied types of objects that were falling from principally German aircraft during the Second phase of the blitz, including high explosives,incendiary bombs and small arms ammunition. Complete with 8 page addendum.

9781783319541

THE MUSKETRY INSTRUCTIONS
FOR THE GERMAN INFANTRY 1887
(Schiessvorshrift fur die Infanterie)
Translated for the intelligence Division War Office

Translated for the War Office by Colonel C W Bowdler Bell

A facsimile that includes the supplement for the German Infantry for 1887. Musketry exercises were intended to give the infantry instruction in shooting, to make effective use of their firearm in battle. As such the manual shows important details designed to make the infantry soldier battle-ready by the end of his first year of service. Instruction is subdivided into Preparatory exercises; Target practice; Field firing; Instructional firing; Inspection in musketry; Proving the rifle M/61.84 and revolver M/83. Many black powder weapons were still used, mainly for training purposes, up to end of the First World War.

9781783313631